Come Walk With An Empath

*I am here to share the rawness of my soul
as I express it through my poetry*

April Wolstencroft *alw*

Contents

Title Page	
My Therapy	1
Come Walk With An Empath	2
Confusion	3
Synchronicity	4
The Search For My Authentic Self	5
Enjoy The Change	6
What Do I Fear?	7
Transformation	9
Let Me Heal You With My Light	11
Are You Awake?	12
Delicious Ambiguity	13
A Crack To The Soul	14
I Dance Differently	15
Empaths Are United	16
Another Test	18
A Curse	19
Our Quest	20
I Am Not Here For Me, I Am Here For You	21
A Storm Is Only A Moment In Time	23

She Found A Narcissist	24
Law Of Attraction	26
Retrograde	27
I Am Me	28
Oneness	30
My Freedom	31
Empowered Empath	32
Be	33
Healer	34
Spiritual Family	35
Dark Night Of The Soul	36
Victory	37
About The Author	39

My Therapy

∞∞∞

This piece of paper, my best friend.
This pen, my therapist.
I break down my mind
Only when the pen hits the paper
And my hands freely scribble words
That may only ever be understood by myself.
It's the only way I can keep
This chaotic mind of mine
In order.

Come Walk With An Empath

∞∞∞

Do not fear what you cannot see
For the universe has guided you
Directly to me
Your confused,
Let me explain
I possess a rather remarkable gift
Misunderstood by many
My abilities excel
In the depths of your darkness
As I walk through your aura
Taking on your struggles
Allowing your pain to feed my soul
I immediately understand you
Will you trust me enough
To rid you from this darkness
Hold my hand
Let's take a walk
As we converse until you see your light

Confusion

∞∞∞

I can't break it down
Frustrated
Complicated
A million thoughts a minute
I can't even keep up with one
I don't like this chaotic mess
I can't stand this confusion
I like simplicity
But there isn't any right now

Synchronicity

∞ ∞ ∞

Step back,
Step out,
And look around
Focus on the world around
Rather the life I am living
Stop and look at the signs
Are they guiding me?

The Search For My Authentic Self

∞ ∞ ∞

This complexity
This confusion
This chaos
I like calmness
But I cannot seem to find any
I must have lost my path
And somehow got lost in the depths of life
My tranquility is somewhere
I just cannot seem to see past the fogginess of my horizon
Is it so far gone?
Making it unreachable?
It cannot be too late
To rediscover it
I must selflessly depart
Leaving those behind
My journey is only equipped for two
So, Me and my shadow
Must travel lightly
Back through the rough
Let me take a deep breath
For this turn around will be full of exhaustion
But I need to find my authentic self
It is the alignment to my calm

Enjoy The Change

∞∞∞

In this world
You have those who find their strength
And those that give up
When you're at a point in your life
Where you feel lost
Don't be the one who gives up
All you may need is just a different course
Stop the need to please
And focus on yourself
Step off your current comfortable path
As it no longer serves you
Conquer this fear of change
Embark on a new course
Some may not follow
Just let them go
Believe in yourself
Take the first step
Enjoy the change
It will lead you to freedom.

What Do I Fear?

∞∞∞

Hello.
Shocked?
Did you assume me to speak of spiders, heights or even the dark?
Ha, I laugh, because those are simple words used
to define the normal things people fear.
But me, I fear Hello.
Silly you say,
As its just a word used to greet another.
So how can one word bring such fear to my soul?
In order to understand my fear, you must understand why.
The way the term is used, is not my fear.
It's the actions followed by the term that awakens it
For every Hello spoken, a good bye follows
It may not be immediate
It may be for a simple reason
Or an inevitable life situation
But eventually you will mutter Good bye
So understand this fear
Embrace it how you choose
But know, As you speak Hello to me today,
Internally I am fighting my fear
Hoping you are not just a part in my current chapter
Trying to keep a positive light
But it fades quickly
As my fear continues to control the deepest parts of me
For hellos are left with good byes
And I am left in a disturbed solitude
as my own voices scream in my head
Questioning why

APRIL WOLSTENCROFT

So no, I am not like others who fear the normal things
I fear Hello.

Transformation

∞ ∞ ∞

She breaks.
The girl that was able to stand, falls.
The girl that was able to carry burdens, weakens.
The girl that was able to live amongst cruelty, submits.
The girl that everyone knew, says good bye.
May she, as we knew her, rest in peace...
Wait,
She's entering into a different dimension
What's this awareness to her soul
The burdens, the cruelty, the weakness,
merges into one form; Her
It was like a veil lifted to a new world
Strangely, every unsettling situation was given a reason
She sat confused, but still allowing her imaginal
cells continue to form wings
Scared only because she can not see
But fear she does not sense
What is she becoming?
Will she love deeper?
Will she trust stronger?
Will she be beautiful?
What a beautiful voice she hears
Its calming her anxieties
"Stop referring to yourself as she
It is you", it says
You are your beautiful voice you hear
My soul I hear you.
I am molding into the rarest form
A transformation similar to the caterpillar and the butterfly

APRIL WOLSTENCROFT

I am not afraid now
Let me see my new transformation
Opening my eyes
I have entered this world as a new species
I feel so powerful as I spread my wings
I feel so free
As I soar through this new world founded by me.

Let Me Heal You With My Light

∞∞∞

I see tears in your eyes, I tell her.
But I am not crying, she says.
Maybe not to the naked eye,
But my dear, I can see your soul
And you are in pain
Hold my hand
Share your story
You are not alone
Let me heal you with my light.

He says, I am fine.
I am sorry, my friend I can hear the truth in your broken voice
And your status is not fine
Hold my hand
Do not fear to share your truth
You are not alone,
Let me heal you with my light.

Stranger, do you need help?
No, they say.
Forgive me, but I instantly feel the instability deep within you
You do not need to share, for your world is not part of mine
But, you are part of this universe
And stranger or not,
Here is my light
You are not alone.

Are You Awake?

∞∞∞

Close your eyes
Inhale
Hold your breath
Let the emotions break through your cortex
Feeding your limbic system
As if they are its only form of survival
Feel the anger, sadness, regret, fear, misery, anxiety, resentment, egoism…
Allow your body to break it down
Turning the dark into its natural light
Essentially expanding your souls' energy
Now exhale
Do you feel the happiness, joy, contentment, serenity, relief, altruism?
Open your eyes
Are you awake?

Delicious Ambiguity

∞ ∞ ∞

Dear child;
What is it that you ask?
Of course, we are connected
I am your universe
I am your vibration
I am the higher power
Waiting for your disconnection
Until then I keep you connected
To my frequencies
Don't you feel them?
Your whispers confirm you do
Scream your words
Do not hide
Empower your internal gift
Share your light.

What is it that you ask?
No, my child I will not teach you
I am here to only love you
Why, you ask?
Because love will ultimately teach you
Continue to question your purpose
The answers are only found in the tomorrows
But the questions must be asked today
Trust in your existence
As it has a purpose
Your reality is real
Live it through your light.

A Crack To The Soul

∞∞∞

When darkness strikes suddenly
And weakens you
Breaking you down
As you feel a piece of your reality become disconnected
A loss that reaches deeper then your surface
It's the loss that doesn't just break your heart
But cracks your soul
Can you find your strength to shine your light?

I Dance Differently

∞∞∞

Stop trying to fix me
I'm only broken to you
I am not different
I just dance differently
Stop making excuses
It's you who has the insecurities
I'm happy being me
I live in a world that seeks imperfection
Where beauty wakes in the dark
Where different shines with acceptance
And weakness is not a disguise.
A utopia, maybe
Like I said
I dance differently.

My mind has triggers
I wish you would see
I try to find the words to explain
But would you understand if they were found?
Maybe my actions will send some clarity.

Never mind,
I'm happy being me,
So just take my hand
Let's just dance
But remember
I dance differently.

Empaths Are United

∞∞∞

Unable to predict the future
I stand in fear
With an unsettling feeling in the pit of my stomach
I have felt this before
The days from my past
That filled with anxiety
Is there anyone else out there that feels this
I know I am not alone
For I feel their fear as well
Your words do not speak
But they never needed to in the presence of me
I vibrate with your frequencies
And your eyes are galactic
As they travel me through your reality
Allowing me to feel your ever so true emotions
See, you stand in fear too
And seek acceptance
From the already conditioned perception of you and me
Lets break this cycle
Lets join together
And vibe as one
The universe has plans for us
Lets answer her vibrations
And use the powers within us

Lets face our fears
Lets reach ascension
Lets change their perception

We are not just one
We are many
For the truth lays in our future;

EMPATHS ARE UNITED.

Another Test

∞∞∞

Difficulties arise
During unpredictable times
Opening the dark doors
Attempting to dim ones light
Questioning this mental stability
Planting seeds of fear
Knowing if watered
They have the ability to grow
Into a forest of misery
Fear a natural emotion
Powerful if felt
As it becomes a thief in the night
Stealing ones emotional clarity
But I am more powerful
Watering this seed with hope
It will sprout into a garden of solitude
Because hope is too a natural emotion
Much more powerful than fear
And ultimately will conquer all
So My light will stay shining bright
While I pass this test my universe has given me.

A Curse

∞∞∞

A Curse
That has me losing myself in others
But finding my oneness with the universe
I absorb all of you
Your pain
Your trauma
Your sadness
Your soul
I channel it
I crave such a connection
For healing you
Strangely heals me
A curse so beautiful
It empowers me.

Our Quest

∞∞∞

We set forth
Lost on a quest
To find our own being
Asking questions
Saying prayers
Hoping the answer comes in black and white
Pain, trauma, sadness strikes
Changing our voyage
Down a path of darkness
Now closing our vision
Giving up on our reasons
No longer lost on a quest
But more so lost in the fear of these emotions
Running now
Running from the greatest opportunity For at this moment
Our questions
Our prayers
Are being answered
But fear forces us to ignore
Because the answers didn't come in our wanted form
But these emotions that arise
They are indeed
The gateway to our soul
Guiding us on the path to the infinite.

I Am Not Here For Me, I Am Here For You

∞ ∞ ∞

She provides my purpose
She sends me people
That are wandering
Lifelessly
In and out of realms
I am not here for me,
I am here for you.

You are lost
Broken
Close to disaster
Don't question how I know this
Because you are not quite ready
To hear my truth
As you linger too long
In your current truth.

Show yourself
Don't hide behind the misconception of vulnerability
Trust me
I am not here for me,
I am here for you.

There you are
I hear your thoughts

Through your movements
You're finally welcoming me
You're leaving your world
Ready to accept your fate

Fearless forms
Now you're ready to hear my truth
I am a healed light
Constantly shining brighter for those to see
I enhance their confidence
Allowing them to believe
Their own powers
Their true gifts
Their true destiny
So you see
I was never here for me,
I was always here for you.

A Storm Is Only A Moment In Time

∞ ∞ ∞

A storm of darkness
Floods your gates
Pushing you back
Forcing waves of pain
Thrashing against your mind
Weakening your stance
These gusts of emotions
Feel like razor blades on a mission
To break through your outer core
In efforts to bleed your soul
As you fight to survive
Are you strong enough to withstand
The unbearable currents of this storm?
Wait!
Did you fail to recall
A storm is only a moment in time
While you are endless
Electrify your light
Shock the pain
Ride the waves
Save your soul
Empower your purpose.

She Found A Narcissist

∞ ∞ ∞

An empath found a narcissist
Pausing for a minute
Her vision unclear
Lost in her mind
Reality a glare
Her confidence so distant
Her confusion arising
How did the tables turn?
The words they whispered
Spoken with such confidence
Broke through her guarded walls
Releasing doubts of herself
Convincing her to believe the lies
Breaking her down
But they saw her inner strength
So in fear of losing her
They would reach out their hands
To comfort her
Holding her close
Only to inject her with venom
From the needles their hands hid
Attempting to weaken her existence
What they never saw
Was the warrior within
Who fed on the venom
As it strengthened her soul
Breathing out fire
And standing tall
She walked out her body

Covered in ash
Beware to all
The Narcissist did not survive
For the empath rose with fire in her veins.

Law Of Attraction

∞∞∞

What you speak you attract
In summary that's the law of attraction
So if I raise my vibrations to protect myself
To shield my energy
Because I fear depletion
Is the law of attraction working in my negative favor
In which I am actually turning what I think is a protective wall
Into a magnetic field
Which is then attracting the negative vibes I fear
Let me save myself
And reverse this
Let me wake up my empowerment
As I step out into this battlefield of unstable energies
Breathing in my surroundings
Let me face this
Let me fully embrace the purest of me

Retrograde

∞∞∞

My struggles consume me
As they wreak havoc
Causing an internal imbalance
From the release of toxins
Absorbed by my mind
Forcing myself
Into retrograde
To disable this weakness
And seek the remedy to my struggles
I must believe
I must believe in myself
I must believe in my struggles
I must believe in the universe
As she strategically works
To revamp my spiritual path
Allowing room
For the redesigning of my rejuvenated soul.

I Am Me

∞∞∞

I do not allow the words written through a book
Define my empathy
I am me
I am oneness
I feel deeply
I read vibrations of all sorts
I focus on your eyes
I read your soul through them
I am full of various gifts
Most described through the context in which I read
But I do not define myself through them
Meditation is not my forte.
I reach my oneness through my own calm
I know how deep my soul connects
I cleanse my aura with the connections to my spiritual zones
Others never understood my compassion
Or my immediate actions of forgiveness
My spiritual journey has left me often on my own
Its an awoken territory
Guarded by my energies
Enemies attempt to enter
They set up fort with their strategies
To wreak havoc on my untouched sanctuary
In hopes of destroying my peace
Wishing to break my spirit
But learning rather quickly
When they lose the battle
How protected my sacred ground is

A warning to all
Who choose to enter
Proceed at your own risk
You will not break me
For I am awake
Vibrating on the highest of frequencies
Even when misunderstood
Even if alone

Oneness

∞∞∞

My soul harmonizes to the sounds around me
My vision sees the depths of others emotional states
I am not a label
I vibrate on various frequencies
No expectations
No judgements
I am my own truth
Fully connected to the universe
I am oneness

My Freedom

∞ ∞ ∞

I sat close to danger
Flirted with the sins of my thoughts
My mind became my prison
That was ruled by demons
A constant burning existence to hell
Fear became my survival tactic
Weakening my reasons to escape
Playing victim with the chains that caged me
No visitors in sight
Exhaustion became my power
I became my purpose
My mind turned and became my savior
My darkness broke my chains
And with the power of a simple flame
My freedom became my light

Empowered Empath

∞∞∞

I am an empath
Gifts of all ability
Uniqueness so pure
Spirituality enlightened
Intuition so clear
An awakened third eye
I feed from the universe
I learn from myself
My surroundings encompass me
Feeling emotions from all sources
Maturation in my shielding
Thriving in my existence
Beautifying my gifts
Standing proudly
As an empowered empath

Be

∞∞∞

In a world full of darkness, be light.
In a world full of sadness, be joy.
In a world full of ugly, be kind.
In a world full of chaos, be calm.
In a world full of toxicity, be cleansed.
In a world full of lost, be found.
In a world full of fake, be real.
In a world full of hate, be love.
In a world full of woke, be awake.
In a world full of others, be you.

Healer

∞ ∞ ∞

I've searched beyond the measures of my own existence
Failed many times at discovering my truth
Lost sight of my own vision
From the darkness felt within
I know pain
I know loss
I know loneliness
It's made me weak to existing
Believing in my wishful demise
Resulting in flight
Getting lost in the maze
Going crazy with nothing but mirrors being forced upon me
Forcing me to see
Surrendered to the acceptance of my beauty
Light pulsated through my veins
My truth brought me home
I discovered my purpose
I awoke to my truth
And now I am here
To heal you.

Spiritual Family

∞∞∞

Weakened to thoughts
Lived through their eyes
With a blinded vision
Speaking words to please others
While I allowed them to control my actions
As if I had strings attached to my body
And I was the star of the puppet show
I became the joke
As I fought to break free
From this robotic version of me
I had a greater power within
Yet my fear kept me hidden
I searched silently
For answers to describe this mockery
My curiosity explored the whispers in the shadows
Breaking me free from these ridiculous strings
I found others as hidden as me
They are my long lost spiritual family.

Dark Night Of The Soul

∞∞∞

It was like a thief in the night
As it broke down the barriers
I worked so hard to build
Without hesitation
It shook my ground
Losing my balance
Weakening my stance
Invading my center
Stealing my light.
Let the truth be told
A thief it was not
I did not put up a fight
I simply allowed my barriers to break down
I actually showed it the way.
This sudden pain forced my soul to escape
And as a defense mechanism
I was the one who hid my light
So my gates can be flooded with this darkness
The expected stay is unknown
All I know, is I must feel it to its entirety
I must allow it to become all of me
And when it's ready to depart
I will understandably send it on its way.

Victory

∞∞∞

The noise broke my silence
As it whispered darkness into my mind
Thoughts invade my peace
Triggers shift my empowerment
Obstructing with my center
Waking up my mental interrogation unit from a long slumber
I'm a warrior with minor weaknesses
And setbacks occasionally occur
My spiritual guidance disappears
As the demons work against them
Faulting me for my weakness
Shaking my foundation
Arousing my inner shift
Expanding my soul
I stand face to face with these demons
Undoubtedly, I am fully equipped for this battle
I slash these demons with 444
Another victory
Darkness is no match for the one who holds light.

About The Author

April Wolstencroft

I have gone through life living in the highest of my own frequencies, unknown of the term empath. And I never did any research on what defines an empath, I just knew I was normal in my own world, but different to some around me. In my younger years, I fought to fit in, but it never ended so great for me. So, I submitted to myself, I allowed the universe to become me. I guided myself through the frequencies of my life and danced to the magnificence of the various gifts given to enhance my beauty.

I feel deeply. I live through my emotions allowing them to create my world around me. I do not fear pain, sadness, or any other form of emotions. I allow them to run through the depths of my soul, where I become them. I interrogate them and when they provide me the answers, I let them go and allow the universe to transmute the energies from them. I allow the emotions of others to enter me, putting a barrier of defense so their energies do not drain me, I bring their emotions to my center and in the moment, I understand their emotional state. I do this for them, so they know they are not alone.

I see the world through the two eyes given to me, but I live in this world through my third eye. I transmute energies through my poetry, and from my soul to yours, I hope my words gave you peace and inspired your empowerment.

Sending love, light and empowerment

April Wolstencroft
alw

www.ingramcontent.com/pod-product-compliance
Lightning Source LLC
Chambersburg PA
CBHW060224050426
42446CB00013B/3162